MARGHERITA LENZINI – EMMA MICHE

# Masterpieces of the
# UFFIZI

**BET**
BONECHI EDIZIONI -IL TURISMO- - FIRENZE

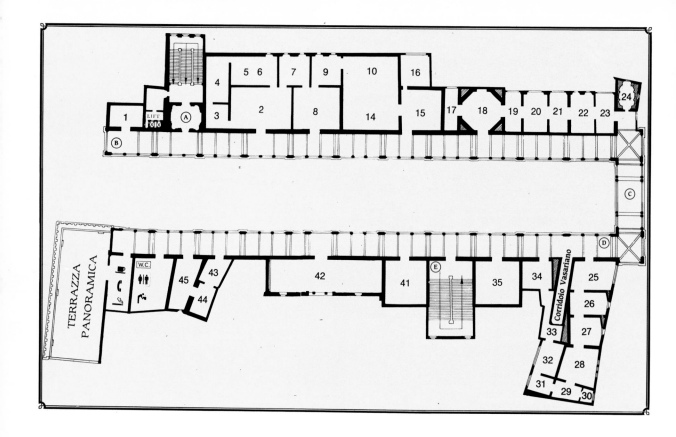

1 – Classical Sculpture.
2 – Giotto and the 13th century.
3 – 14th century Sienese School.
4 – 14th century Florentine School.
5-6 – International Gothic Style.
7 – Early 15th century Florentine School.
8 – Filippo Lippi.
9 – Pollaiolo.
10-14 – Botticelli.
15 – Leonardo da Vinci.
16 – Map Room.
17 – Room of the Hermaphrodite.
18 – The «Tribuna»
19 – Signorelli and Perugino.

20 – Dürer and the German School.
21 – Giovanni Bellini and Giorgione.
22 – Holbein and Altdorfer.
23 – Correggio and Mantegna.
24 – Miniature Collection.
25 – Michelangelo.
26 – Raphael and Andrea del Sarto.
27 – Pontormo.
28 – Titian.
29 – Parmigianino and Central Italian Mannerism.
30 – The Aemilian School.
31 – Dosso Dossi.
32 – 16th century Venetian School.

33 – 16th century Corridor.
34 – Veronese.
35 – Tintoretto and Barocci.
41 – Rubens and van Dyck.
42 – The Niobe Room.
43 – Caravaggio.
44 – Rembrandt, the Flemish and Dutch Masters.
45 – 18th century painting.
A – VESTIBULE AT THE ENTRANCE.
B – FIRST CORRIDOR.
C – SECOND CORRIDOR.
D – THIRD CORRIDOR.
E – EXIT HALL.

© Copyright 1992 by Bonechi Edizioni "Il Turismo" S.r.l
© Copyright 1997 by Bonechi Edizioni "Il Turismo" S.r.l
Via dei Rustici, 5 - 50122 FLORENCE
Tel. +39 (55) 239.82.24/25 - Fax +39 (55) 21.63.66
E-mail address: barbara@bonechi.com / bbonechi@dada.it
Printed in Italy

*Photos*: Bonechi Edizioni "Il Turismo" S.r.l. Archives
*Layout*: Piero Bonechi
*Editing*: Barbara Bonechi
*Typesetting*: Leadercomp, Florence
*Reprohouse*: La Fotolitografia, Florence
*Print*: BO.BA.DO.MA, Florence
**ISBN 88-7204-031-0**

Night view of the Piazzale degli Uffizi.

# THE UFFIZI GALLERY

*Mention was first made of the project for the Uffizi in a letter written by Grandduke Cosimo I to his architect Giorgio Vasari "…I shall be satisfied if the result befits the Association of Magistrates." In fact, the Uffizi was planned as a modern office building in which all the administrative and government offices of the newly-formed Grandduchy of Tuscany would be housed under one roof and its centralizing function and magnificent style would serve to represent the grandeur and unity of the Medicean state.*

*At the time, there were thirteen directors of public administration, heading the department of justice, the guilds, tax offices and the like, with the result that the building was first known as the "Palace of the 13 Magistrates." This name, however, shortly became the Uffizi, which, appropriately enough, means offices.*

*According to document of the time, 234 private homes located between Piazza della Signoria and the Arno River were bought up so a building site could be cleared. As demolitions to make way for the foundations were being*

3

**Self-portrait,** by *Giorgio Vasari*.

**Cosimo I dei Medici,** by *Agnolo Bronzino*.

carried out, even a good part of the Romanesque church of San Piero Scheraggio alongside Palazzo Vecchio was torn down. Today,
remains of San Piero Scheraggio can still be
seen incorporated into the outer wall of the
Uffizi on the Via della Ninna side.

As the letters written back and forth between
Cosimo I and Vasari have been preserved, we
can retrace the progress of the project step by
step. It took only a couple of years to put up the
building, which is an amazingly short time if
you consider the date and size of it.

By 1564 – the walls would be up just a year
later – the so-called "Corridoio Vasariano" join-
ing Palazzo Pitti to Palazzo Vecchio was finished in time for the marriage of Cosimo I's son,
Francesco, to Joan of Austria. The corridoio,
which crosses the Arno River by way of Ponte
Vecchio and has an overhead passageway con-

necting the Uffizi and Palazzo Vecchio, was
Vasari's pride and joy since he managed to
finish it in only five months – rather than the
five years that might have been expected.

After Cosimo's death in 1574, shortly fol-
lowed by Vasari's, Francesco I became Grandduke. One of his wide-ranging interests was the
new building and he had the statues and
paintings belonging to the Medici collections
displayed along the corridors of the loggia, now
entirely glassed-in. Also, he had his collections
of curiosities, weapons, musical instruments,
and jewelry placed in the rooms on either side of
the Tribuna, designed by Buontalenti. These, in
some cases, actually became craftsmen's studios and laboratories, although the experiments
performed in the latter had more to do with
alchemy than chemistry. During this time, too,
the painter Allori and his students were busily

**Francesco I dei Medici,** by *Agnolo Bronzino*.

**Anna Maria Ludovica dei Medici,** by *Jan Frans van Douven*.

engaged in frescoing the so-called "grotesque" designs on the corridor ceilings.

The original collection (which included such masterpieces as Paolo Uccello's Battle of San Romano and Botticelli's Spring and Birth of Venus, just to mention a few of the best known) was constantly expanded through-out the reign of the Medicis, who in the 16th century became granddukes, right up to the time of the last of the dynasty (1737, primarily as a result of the passionate interest all the Medicis took in art). This tradition was continued by the Lorraine granddukes, the Medicis' successors, who went about collecting with just as much intelligence and connoisseurship. Especially worthy of mention is Grandduke Pietro Leopoldo who brought the statues of Niobe and her children up from Rome and had a fine hall built to show them off. Moreover, he had real curators rearrange the gallery collections and opened the museum to the public, both for the first time.

In the 19th century, certain works were removed from the Uffizi to be placed in the more specialized museums then being founded. These new museums included the Archeological Museum (featuring Etruscan and Roman pieces), the Bargello National Museum (sculpture) and later, the Uffizi Prints and Drawings Collections, the Academy Gallery (sculpture and painting) and the San Marco Museum (Fra Angelico).

More recently, new rooms off the East Corridor were turned into galleries and, after World War II, others were added along the West Corridor.

Today, as a result, only sculpture is displayed in the corridors, whereas the paintings are all hung in rooms whose lighting exploits the latest museum developments.

# SAN PIERO SCHERAGGIO

San Piero Scheraggio is the Romanesque church which Vasari had partially torn down and partially incorporated into the huge Uffizi structure.

In 1968-1970 the church's far end and the apse of the nave were restored under the supervision of the Uffizi Superintendent Nello Bemporad. The present-day elevator hall corresponds to what was originally the right aisle, and Via della Ninna to what was once the left one.

Just as its sister Romanesque churches Santi Apostoli and San Miniato, San Piero played an important role in Florentine history. In fact, it was a favorite meeting place for the top-ranking citizens of medieval and republican Florence. One outstanding example is Dante who spoke from its pulpit (now preserved in the church of San Leonardo in Arcetri).

The result of the restoration project is a simple, yet brightly serene, ambience, the effect of which is enhanced by modern functional architectural solutions. Inside the apse the paintings on display include the *Madonna della Ninna*, 14th century Florentine School, which gave the street its name and which perhaps originally hung outside the church itself; a predella by the Florentine painter Giovanni del Biondo (active 1350-1400) illustrating *stories from the life of St. John the Evangelist*, all

that is left of the altarpiece that once adorned the main altar of the original church building.

Along the walls leading to the apse are the frescoes of Famous Men that Andrea del Castagno (c. 1421-1457) painted in c. 1450 for the Carducci-Pandolfini Villa in Legnaia. Detached from the walls of the villa, they were purchased by the Lorraine government in 1852 and for many years displayed in the refectory of Sant'Apollonia. The figures include *Dante*, *Petrach*, *Boccaccio*, *Niccolò Acciaioli*, *Pippo Spano*, and *Farinata degli Uberti*, as well as *Queen Esther*, *Queen Tomiri*, and the *Cumean Sibyl*. The large panel of the *Battle of San Martino* is a modern work of Corrado Cagli. It hangs on the right wall and was donated to the Uffizi in 1983.

New finds turned up during the restoration work: the remains of a sanctuary (probably dating from the Longobard period) which, although inside the crypt itself, is not open to the public, and fragments of Roman walls – perhaps remains of a tavern in the vicinity of the theater which stood nearby.

That the interior was decorated in a highly refined style is shown by the remains of the floral motif frescoes brought to light. The frescoes with animal motifs decorating the windows along the apse evidently date from the Romanesque period.

**Queen Tomiri; Pippo Spano; the Cumaean Sibyl,** three works by *Andrea del Castagno*.

**Apse of San Piero Scheraggio;** below, from left: **Petrarch, Giovanni Boccaccio, Farinata degli Uberti**, three works by *Andrea del Castagno*.

Above: **study of two heads,** by *Leonardo da Vinci*; left: **study of Pallas,** by *Sandro Botticelli*; below: **study of a landscape,** by *Leonardo da Vinci*; facing page: **study of a man's head,** by *Michelangelo*.

# THE PRINTS
# AND DRAWINGS COLLECTION

The Prints and Drawings Collection (Gabinetto dei Disegni e delle Stampe) was started by Cardinal Leopoldo de' Medici in 1675. This collection was housed in Palazzo Pitti until Cosimo III had it moved to the Uffizi and arranged by Filippo Baldinucci. Then in the 18th century it was moved to Buontalenti's Tribune. Later, as the number of works grew and grew, they were temporarily set out in other rooms until their final destination in what had once been the Medici Theater designed by Buontalenti (and destroyed at the end of the 19th century).

The collection was greatly expanded thanks to acquisitions and bequests, until today it totals over 50,000 drawings and 60,000 prints by Italian and non-Italian artists.

Entrance hall; below: the staircase, designed by *Vasari*.

# THE FIRST CORRIDOR

Originally an open loggia atop the Uffizi building, the first corridor is now an extended gallery, constantly alive with steady streams of visitors from all over the world. On either side are Roman sculptures dating from the late Republican and Imperial periods. These include bust of emperor and empresses, statues, and sarcophagi, many of which of great beauty, mainly from the collection of Ferdinando I dei Medici who, before becoming the third grandduke of Tuscany, was a cardinal and thus resided in Rome. The corridor was lined with numerous tapestries. Among these were some of the finest put out by the Florentine works founded by Cosimo I dei Medici: sets of months and "grotesque" motifs designed by Bachiacca, one of the most creative painters of the Florentine Mannerist school. The tapestries have been recently removed for restoration. Also the "grotesque" frescoes on the ceiling inspired by Raphael's Vatican Loggia in Rome are Mannerist works.

The First Corridor; below: detail of a 16th century "grotesque", on the ceiling of the First Corridor.

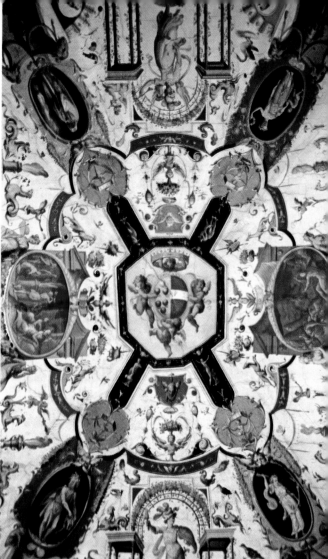

Two details of the frescoes on the ceiling of the First Corridor; below: marble busts of Hadrian, Domitia and Nerva.

**Partial view of the Classical Sculpture Room;** right: **Doriphorus**, Roman copy of a 5th century B.C. Greek original.

# ROOM I (CLASSICAL SCULPTURE)

The main nucleus of the Uffizi classical sculpture collection was assembled by the Medici family during the second half of the 16th century. Cosimo I's passion for Roman art was partly due to his desire to create a parallel between Imperial Rome and the Grandduchy of Tuscany. The Hapsburg-Lorraine family continued to add to the collection, which includes a large number of Roman originals of excellent quality and Imperial Roman copies of Greek originals. Room 1 recently re-opened, used to contain the original panels of the *Ara Pacis*, which were transferred to Rome in the 1920s, when the Ara Pacis was reconstructed.

**Rucellai Madonna,** by *Duccio di Buoninsegna*.

## Cimabue (13th century)

The only documentary evidence we have concerning Cenni di Pepo, better known as Cimabue, dates from 1272, the year he was active in Rome, and the period between 1301-1303 when he was working in Pisa. Nevertheless, art historians have been able to make several definite attributions: the Uffizi Madonna, the frescoes at Assisi, the Crucifixes of Arezzo and Florence, the Louvre Virgin, and the mosaic with St. John of Pisa, to mention the most important.

Originally placed on the main altar of the church of Santa Trinita in Florence, the Uffizi *Maestà* is dated c. 1280, and is thus an early work. The Byzantine tradition, which dominated 13th century Italian art, is evident in the composition and the color scheme, yet a change is apparent in the innovative use of perspective and contour line to create three-dimensional form and the greater, more intimately human, expressiveness of the figures.

## Duccio di Buoninsegna (13th century)

Much is known about the Sienese artist, Duccio, from 1278 to the year of his death, 1319. More closely bound to the Byzantine tradition than his florentine contemporary, Cimabue, Duccio was also influenced by Gothic painting which, by means of easily-transportable illuminated manuscripts, was then widespread in Italy. Duccio, whose style resulted from a harmonious blend of Byzantine and Gothic, was the first to portray the enchanted unreal world tinged with melancholy that is to be found in all of 14th century Sienese painting.

This superb altarpiece is known as the *Rucellai Madonna* since for many years it hung in the Rucellai family chapel in the church of Santa Maria Novella in Florence. For years it was attributed to Cimabue, whose influence, though superficial, is still evident. Nevertheless, the weightless bodies, sinous line, and melancholy faces, Duccio's hallmarks, leave no doubt as to the painter's identity.

Right: **Maestà,** by *Cimabue*.

15

**Annunciation,** by *Simone Martini* and *Lippo Memmi*; opposite: **Virgin enthroned,** by *Giotto*.

## Giotto (1267?-1337)

Tradition has it that Giotto di Bondone, born in Vespignano not far from Florence, was a pupil of Cimabue, later eclipsing the fame of his master. In the words of Dante, his contemporary:

*In painting Cimabue thought he held the field.*
*But now it is Giotto whose crow is louder.*

In fact, Giotto's contemporaries were already aware of the great revolution he had brought about in painting by freeing it from its dependence on Byzantine formulas and treating human figures with a new dignity and solemnity.

This *Virgin enthroned*, originally hung in the church of Ognissanti, in Florence, was painted c. 1310. Ghiberti in his *Commentaries* (15th century) was the first to recognize it as a work of the great master. Even though the whole lacks the cohesive composition and dramatic force of the fresco cycle, the Virgin has been rendered with a three-dimensionality and severity of form hitherto unseen in 14th century painting.

## Simone Martini (c. 1290-1344)

The Sienese painter Simone Martini is the foremost International Style painter in Italy. Duccio, his fellow Sienese, had a great influence on his artistic formation, but most important of all was the influence of French art. In addition to the miniatures then circulating in Italy, he was exposed to other forms of Gothic art when he sojourned at the Court of Robert of Anjou in Naples. He in turn strongly influenced French artists when, in about 1340, he went to Avignon where he left several major works.

The *Annunciation*, a late work signed and dated 1333, originally hung in the Cathedral of Siena. This is one of the most admired painting in Italian art. The ethereal figures caught in rhythmic poses and the decorative details such as the delicately-patterned wings, the flowing cloak, and the lily stalks outlined against the gold ground represent the epitome of refinement and charm. The saints on either side are by Lippo Memmi.

The Thebaid, by *Gherardo Starnina*; below: detail.

## Gherardo Starnina (1354-1413)

Starnina was a loner, perhaps influenced by the Spanish Gothic painting he observed during a documented trip to Spain. Nothing is known of his early training, yet his few extant works (such as the Carmine Church frescoes discovered in 1932 and recently detached) show that his style is comparable to Agnolo Gaddi's i.e. a combination of Giotto's monumental treatment of figures and International Style passion for decorative detail.

The *Thebaid* ostensibly depicts life in an Anachorite hermitage. Actually, though, it illustrates an ideal world, fruit of the artist's imagination, which is peopled with a host of figures set in a minutely-described landscape of craggy cliffs, miniature trees, and waterways. Odd little boats blown by personifications of winds sail along the canal-like river in the eery twilight setting.

## Giottino (14th century)

Hardly any documentary evidence exists about Tommaso di Stefano, better known as Giottino, and in fact for a long time he was even confused with Maso di Banco. Nonetheless, Giottino, one of Giotto's most talented and faithful followers, has a definite personality of his own. Many of his stylistic characteristics, such as his palette dominated by blended tones, delicate touches of shading, and his close attention to drapery details, would seem to reveal a modern background. He might very well have been from Lombardy (Giotto, in fact, lived the last years of his life in Milan), although he is believed to have been active primarily in Tuscany.

Originally hung in the Florentine church of San Remigio (near Piazza Signoria), this *Deposition* was attributed to Giottino by Vasari who went on to describe the figures "who, with infinite sorrow and tender loving gestures, mourn His death." The horizontal composition, emphasized by the recumbant figure of Christ and the cross-bar, is attained by the rhythmic arrangement of the figures around the dead Christ.

Right: **Deposition**, by *Giottino*.

18

19

**Adoration of the Magi,** by *Lorenzo Monaco*.

# Lorenzo Monaco (1370-1425)

Lorenzo Monaco, although a Sienese by birth, lived in the Monastery of Santa Maria degli Angeli in Florence where he was a friar in the Camaldolese order. His style has much of the International Style decorativeness, yet it differs in that it has more subdued religiosity and contemplativeness. Monaco derived his passion for enamel-like colors of contrasting hues from a study of miniatures, while his use of gold grounds is a clear sign of his Sienese backgrounds. His delicate line is soft and flowing, although at times he does tend to get calligraphic. Lastly, his entire oeuvre, small painting and huge altarpieces, as well as frescoes, reveals a consistent, non-evolutive style throughout.

The *Adoration of the Magi* was painted for the church of San Marco in Florence, probably c. 1420. Despite the fact that he has accurately portrayed the figures crowding the Virgin and Child, he gives in to the temptation of minutely describing their exotic drapery and the elegant dogs and horses in the best International Style fashion. The whole scene is bathed in an otherworldly magical light which highlights the shepherds in the background, the mountains, and the soft, contrasting colors, just as we find in illuminated manuscripts.

**Coronation of the Virgin,** by *Lorenzo Monaco*.

**Adoration of the Magi,** by *Gentile da Fabriano*.

## Gentile da Fabriano (1360-1427)

Gentile, born in Fabriano (Umbria), studied painting first in Umbria and the nearby Marche, and then in Northern Italy where he came into contact with Venetian and Lombard artists steeped in the International Style. Gentile's major undertakings, namely the frescoes in Venice and Brescia, have not come down to us but, among the few surviving works that have, are the two paintings in the Uffizi.

This splendid *Adoration*, painted for the Strozzi Chapel in the church of Santa Trinita in Florence, is signed and dated 1423. The artist has given free rein to his lively imagination. The entourage of elaborately-costumed figures winds its way over hill and dale down to the lower lefthand corner where the Holy Family, rendered with delicacy of color and form, has been relegated (the figures of the Virgin and the Babe and the two ladies-in-waiting behind them are especially charming). The whole composition gravitates towards the elegant figure of the youngest blond-haired Magus placed in the middle foreground.

**Coronation of the Virgin,** by *Fra Angelico*.

## Fra Giovanni Angelico (c. 1400-1455)

After finishing his religious training at the Dominican Monastery in Fiesole, Fra Angelico became an artist, starting out as a manuscript illuminator and then as a painter and frescoist. Although his early works still retain something of the delicate moment of transition represented by Masolino and the sculptor Ghiberti, he was primarily influenced by Masaccio. In fact, his deep involvement with Renaissance innovations is revealed by his skillful use of perspective. He places his figures in believable three-dimensional settings, be they cloistered gardens, plain monastic cells, or just simple gold grounds. Indeed, despite the mystical quality of their poses and color, his figures are rendered as solid bodies in space.

This *Coronation of the Virgin* was painted between 1430 and 1435. The Renaissance use of perspective is evident in the treatment of the heavenly choir of angels and saints which curves into the background. At the same time, the elongated figures, delicate blended colors, and gold ground convey an effect of harmonius serenity.

**The Battle of San Romano,** by *Paolo Uccello*; opposite: **Virgin and Child with St. Anne,** by *Masolino* and *Masaccio*.

## Masolino (1383-1447) – Masaccio (1401-1428)

These two painters represent the two different tendencies of Italian art which prevailed during the first twenty years of the 15th century. On one hand, Masolino never broke away from the International Style and did his best work outside Florence (poetic fresco cycles in Castiglione Olona in Lombardy and San Clemente in Rome). Masaccio, on the other hand, along with Brunelleschi in architecture and Donatello in sculpture, is considered one of the creators of the Florentine Renaissance. During the Renaissance revolution, the technical problems relating to light and perspective and the heroic nature of man were solved.

Masaccio's frescoes in the Brancacci Chapel in the Carmine Church in Florence represent the highpoint of his art, the final result of a search begun with this *Virgin and Child*. Masolino, commissioned to paint it for the church of Sant'Ambrogio in Florence, put in the figures of St. Anne and all the angels, except for the green-gowned one on the right. This figure he left to his pupil Masaccio, along with that of the Virgin. She is enclosing the Babe, as solid as any of Donatello's sculpted cherubs, like a human niche.

## Paolo Uccello (1397-1475)

Trained in the International Style, Paolo Uccello soon became passionately involved in the new Renaissance movement. He was especially fascinated by problems of perspective, as we can clearly see from this painting which abounds in geometric forms placed in various picture planes, *mazzocchi* shown from all angles, and bold head-on foreshortening views. This involvement with perspective, sometimes carried to the point of absurdity, is evident in all his works, from the frescoed equestrian monument of John Hawkwood in the Florence Cathedral to the frescoes in the Chiostro Verde in Santa Maria Novella (Florence) depicting stories from the life of Noah.

The *Battle of San Romano* was probably painted for Cosimo the Elder. Dated 1456-1457, it is one of a set of three (the other two ended up in the Louvre and National Gallery in the 19th century). Here the artist uses a profusion of broken lances and impossible foreshortened views of the rounded horses to create a thrilling fantasy world all his own. An almost magical light deadens the action creating a pattern effect reminiscent of oversize pieces in a fabulous puzzle.

**Virgin and Child with saints,** or **St. Lucy Altarpiece,** by *Domenico Veneziano.*

# Domenico Veneziano (active 1438-1461)

Little is known about this painter and likewise little of his oeuvre has come down to us. Born in Venice as his name indicates, he undoubtedly was influenced by the Gothic style prevalent in northern Italy, especially in the use of color. In 1438 he wrote to Piero dei Medici to offer his services. Undoubtedly his artistic education was based on the Gothic world of the north with its enchanting colors. Then in Florence he came into contact with Masolino, and the Renaissance painters, and both strains are harmoniously blended in his mature works.

This painting, also known as the *St. Lucy Altarpiece,* was painted for the church of Santa Lucia dei Magnoli and is signed and dated 1445. One of Veneziano's major works, and fundamental for an understanding of his oeuvre, the painting shows the Virgin holding the Babe, surrounded by Sts. Francis, John the Baptist, Zenobius, and Lucy. The figures, reminiscent of Luca and Andrea della Robbia's sculpture, are harmoniously placed in an architectural setting of light-colored marble arches and niches. The use of perspective and spatial composition is quite remarkable, as is the color scheme which conveys an intensely throbbing luminous effect.

**Portraits of Battista Sforza** and **Federico da Montefeltro,** both by *Piero della Francesca*; below:
**Federico's Triumph,** on the back of the portrait.

# Piero della Francesca (1416-1492)

Born in Sansepolcro (south Tuscany) Piero definitely came into contact with both Umbrian and Sienese art, deriving from the latter his brand of International Style ecstatic enchantment. In Florence, as a pupil of Domenico Veneziano, he adopted his master's clear bright lighting and set out on the study of perspective, with the result that he soon achieved a perfect synthesis of form and color. In addition, the influence of Flemish painting gave a pearly luster to his palette. His unique vision, at the same time abstract and profoundly introverted, is epitomized in the Story of the True Cross fresco cycle in the church of San Francesco in Arezzo, although it is also present in all his works.

These *portraits of the Duke and Duchess of Urbino, Federico da Montefeltro* and *Battista Sforza*, with allegories of their *triumphs* on the back, were painted in 1465-1466. The landscapes reaching back behind the figures, especially in the Duke's portrait, are bathed in a clear glow which makes the water and sky appear almost transparent.

Four works by *Filippo Lippi*. Above: **Adoration of the Child with St. John and St. Romualdus**; left: **Adoration of the Child with St. Hilarion**; below: **Virgin enthroned with saints**; right **Virgin and Child with two angels**.

## Filippo Lippi (c. 1406-1469)

A Carmelite friar as well as a painter, Filippo Lippi, from the outset of his artistic career was influenced by the art of Masaccio and actively took part in the creation of the Florence Renaissance. In his work, Masaccio's simple monumentality and Fra Angelico's mysticism are blended to create an effect of joyful domesticity. His palette is full and rich, at times expressing an almost romantic lyricism. While this romantic lyrical strain runs throughout his whole oeuvre, as he drew farther from Masaccio's influence, his forms become lighter and airier.

One of his most celebrated paintings, this charming *Virgin and Child* is a late work dated c. 1464. The treatment of light is the outstanding feature of the painting: entering from the window framing the Virgin in the foreground and a far-reaching landscape beyond, the light delicately models the figures, caressing the Virgin's fine, chiselled profile and softening the Babe's fleshy solidity. A touch of reality is admirably achieved by the mischievous grin on the face of the foreground angel who turns towards the viewer as if in search of his fair share of attention.

Three works by *Antonio del Pollaiolo*. Above: **Hercules slaying the Hydra**; right: **Hercules strangling Anteus**; below: **Portrait of a Lady**.

## Antonio del Pollaiolo (1429-1498)

Antonio del Pollaiolo started out as a goldsmith and, in addition to being a painter, was also a great sculptor of bronzes. While he lacks Domenico Veneziano's ecstatic approach to art and Piero della Francesca monumentality, he is an outstanding draughtsman, using line as a way of achieving an effect of vigorous movement. As a result, especially in his painting, a hidden source of impetuous vitaly throbs beneath the splendor of his vibrant color, at times bursting forth in a frenetic explosion of vital force.

This dynamism in perfectly revealed in this *Hercules strangling Anteus* and its companion piece *Hercules slaying the Hydra* which were stolen from the museum and recovered in the United States in 1963. The tremendous effort put forth by Hercules as he attempts to crush his enemy is expressed through the use of outline. The harsh nervous line galvanizes them into action, transmissing to their bodies a sense of dramatic intensity. The extended landscape acts as a kind of visual echo, reflecting waves of the desperate struggle all the way back to the reaches of the horizon line, giving the whole a cosmic resonance.

**Madonna del Magnificat,** by *Sandro Botticelli*.

# THE BOTTICELLI HALL

The results of in-depth museum studies, the new Botticelli Hall was opened to the public in 1978. The Botticelli here range from the painter's more resplendent to his more reflective period when he became a follower of Savonarola's preachings. Other master represented are Hugo van der Goes (the huge Portinari Altarpiece), Rogier van del Weyden (Deposition), Filippino Lippi, and Domenico Ghirlandaio. One of the first things that strikes you as you enter is the size of the hall, the biggest in the Uffizi.Once it was the far side of the Medici Theater which originally took up a large chunk of the gallery, going right up to the second floor. Actually, this room was the upper part of the stage and in fact during restoration the original beams were brought to light (one dating from 1623 is known to have been put in to replace an earlier defective one). The effect of grandeur and monumentality of the hall is attained by the huge beams. The Medici Theater, Buontalenti's masterpiece, was inaugurated in 1589. It was a modern theater with stepped seats adorned with columns and statues (one of which is now at the bottom of the staircase leading up to the museum), and the orchestra sloping down to the stage to which it was connected by two little staircases. Famous plays were performed here. Buontalenti himself acted as

**Madonna of the Pomegranate;** opposite: **Coronation of the Virgin,** both by *Sandro Botticelli.*

choreographer, set designer (there were even moving sets), and director. We might even say that Italian melodrama started on its conquest of the world from this very theater. The fame of the spectacles, especially those put on as part of the extravagant festivities for marriages in the Medici family, spread throughout Europe. An engraving by Jacques Callot dated c. 1617 shows the theater decked out in all its splendor. Theater was a great passion with practically all of the Medici princes who spent their time and money on it. Later on Great Prince Ferdinando commissioned an open-air theater to be built on the grounds of his villa in Pratolino. Ferdinando, patron of Alessandro Scarlatti, Frederick Haendel, and benefactor of Bartolommeo Cristofari, inventor of the piano, composed the work "The Greek in Troy" especially for this theater.

## Sandro Botticelli (1445-1510)

Heir to Pollaiolo's functional style, Botticelli turns Antonio's throbbing tension into almost musical rhythm, attaining the height of expression in the mythological paintings of his mature period. In fact, early in his career he moved into the Medicis' cicle of Humanist intellectuals which numbered thinkers of the stature of Marsilio Ficino, Agnolo Poliziano, and Lorenzo the Magnificent among its members. As a result, it was not long before Botticelli's art reflected the literary, philosophical and mythological themes exalting the intelligence and perfection of man dear to the Humanists. His early paintings in fact reveal his constant striving to attain pure beauty, until becoming a follower of the ascetic monk Savonarola brought him to more sombre reflections and soul-searching. This is reflected in the harsher, more austere style of his later years,

**Portrait of an unknown man with a medallion;** opposite: **Pallas and the Centaur;** following
pages: **Allegory of Spring,** three works by *Sandro Botticelli.*

Above: **Flora**; left: **the three Graces**, details from the **Allegory of Spring**, by *Sandro Botticelli*; following pages: **Birth of Venus**, by *Sandro Botticelli*.

Calumny; below: **detail of the Adoration of the Magi,** both by *Sandro Botticelli*; left: **detail of Venus,** from the Birth of Venus, by *Sandro Botticelli*.

permeated with a tremor of tragic desperation. Painted for Lorenzo di Pierfrancesco dei Medici in 1477-1478, the *Allegory of Spring* is acclaimed as one of the artist's masterpieces. It is at the same time the most complete and perfect expression of his mature painting style and his Platonic Humanist ideals relating to pure beauty. In this painting, inspired by Poliziano's *Stanze*, the Classical world of Ovid and Lucretius is filtered and transformed into Botticelli's charmed lyricism. The name of the famous work was given by Vasari in the 16th century. Of later date, probably just after the completion of the frescoes Botticelli did in the Sistine Chapel in the Vatican in 1481-1482, is the tondo known as the *Madonna del Magnificat*, which until 1675 was part of Cardinal Leopold dei Medici's private collection. Exhibiting a masterful blend of lovely colors, palpable forms, and charming landscape, this work marks the beginning of what we may perhaps term Botticelli's most classical period. One of the most effective and imaginative touches is the embrace of the angels who thus create a second dynamic frame within the actual picture frame itself.

Botticelli, then at the peak of his creative powers, soon went on (c. 1486) to paint the *Birth of Venus* commissioned by Lorenzo di Pierfrancesco dei Medici. Botticelli pictures Venus just as she is coming to life, carried ashore by the concerted huffing and puffing of the Zephyr winds.

**Portinari Altarpiece,** by *Hugo van der Goes*; below: **the central panel.**

**Detail of the Shepherds,** from the central panel of the Portinari Altarpiece, by *Hugo van der Goes*; below: **the central panel.**

# Hugo van der Goes (c. 1440-1482)

Probably a native of Ghent, Flanders, where we find him a member of the painters' guild in 1467, Hugo van der Goes greatly enriched Flemish painting. He brought to it a new, highly complex compositional scheme and monumentality, setting his religious scenes in far-reaching, richly-tinted landscapes. A non-conformist in both his artistic and private lives, van der Goes devoted his multiple energies to various aspects of painting, including experimenting with different techniques and elaborating new themes. Shortly after 1478, he retired from everyday life becoming a lay brother in the Cloître Rouge near Brussels, where he died four years later.

Unfortunately, much of his Belgian work was destroyed during the Iconoclast uprising of 1575, but his most important work, the *Portinari Altarpiece*, commissioned by Tommaso Portinari, the Medicis' agent in Bruges, was executed for the main altar of the church of Sant'Egidio in Florence and thus has come down to us intact. Painted in 1476-1479, the altarpiece was much admired in Florence and greatly influenced several well-known Florentine artists of the day.

45

**Deposition,** by *Rogier van der Weyden.*

# Rogier van der Weyden (c. 1400-1464)

First mentioned in a document dated 1427, van der Weyden was a pupil of the Flemish master, Robert Campin. Stylistically related to the celebrated van Eyck brothers, his work is nevertheless fraught with greater dynamism and vigor, a result of van der Weyden's exposure to Italian painting in 1449-1450 when he visited Ferrara, Florence and Rome on occasion of a trip for the Holy Year celebration.

In fact, it is very likely that this *Deposition*, formerly in the Medici Villa in Careggi, was painted during that time. Similar in subject matter and composition to a Fra Angelico now in the Munich Art Museum, it is nevertheless quite different stylistically. Van der Weyden's emphasis on naturalistic and anatomical detail is in sharp contrast to Fra Angelico's lyrical, more abstract rendering.

**Adoration of the Magi,** by *Domenico Ghirlandaio*.

## Domenico Ghirlandaio (1449-1494)

Although Ghirlandaio was evidently influenced by Masaccio's tactile values, Pollaiolo's dynamism, and Verrocchio's skillful use of light, he watered down their great dramatic force by using overly bright colors and crowds of graceful portrait figures in a whole series of works that are nevertheless faithful illustrations of 15th century Florentine society. Despite the fact that he lacked great psycho-

logical insight, he became the foremost illustrator of his times, making the ostensible religious scenes he frescoed in the churches of Santa Maria Novella and Santa Trinita faithful views of the people and places of 15th century Florence.

In this *Adoration of the Magi*, Ghirlandaio describes the personages and costumes of his day, updating the storybook world of his illustrious predecessors, Gentile da Fabriano, Domenico Veneziano and Benozzo Gozzoli, by a use of vaster perpective and more solid forms.

49

**Portrait of Benedetto Portinari,** by *Hans Memling*.

# Hans Memling (c. 1433-1494)

Although Memling was actually from Mainz, Germany, his style is more Flemish than German, due to the fact that he studied under the great Fleming Rogier van der Weyden and took up residence in Bruges, Flanders. Purposely more archaic than his master, Memling's poetic style, especially in small religious pictures, is characterized by delicate figures set in delightful landscapes revealing a pronounced innate love of nature. His portraits are rightly ranked among the finest of all Flemish painting.

Here *Benedetto Portinari* (son of Tommaso Portinari who commissioned the celebrated Portinari Altarpiece) is shown in prayer, an expression both gentle and absorbed on his face and his hands joined over his open prayer book to create an effect of intimate religiosity. The portrait dated 1487 is a late work.

**Adoration of the Magi,** by *Andrea Mantegna*.

# Andrea Mantegna (1431-1506)

Mantegna, a native of Padua, was influenced by both the Florentine school (he knew the works Donatello, Andrea del Castagno, Paolo Uccello, and Filippo Lippi had executed in his native city) and the Venetian school, through contact with the Bellini family, the famous painters from Venice. This dual influence had an attenuating effect on his original, strictly Classical formation, so that his rather cold revocations of Antiquity were softened into a more human, more natural approach.

The *Adoration of the Magi* is the center panel of a triptych whose wings with scenes of the Circumcision and the Ascension are believed to have been painted at different times. The scene of the Adoration probably dates from 1467, shortly after the artist's stay in Florence, when he came into contact with Lorenzo the Magnificent's court and drew inspiration from the technical and compositional innovations he was exposed to.

The Tribuna; below: **detail of the dome of the Tribuna;** opposite: **the Medici Venus,** Hellenistic copy of a 4th century B.C. original.

# THE "TRIBUNA"

This octagonal room, built by Buontalenti for Francesco I in 1589, reflects the splendid taste of the Mannerist period. An attempt has been made to restore it to its original refined splendor. The walls lined in red silk represent, just as the original velvet covering did, fire, one of the four elements which make up the allegorical scheme of the room. Above glows the mother-of-pearl dome symbolizing water, lit up by the lantern with winds symbolizing air. The flame red walls are reflected in the geometric green and white floor which certainly represents earth. The huge *table* inlaid with semi-precious stones was crafted in the Medicis' own workshop. Designed by Jacopo Ligozzi especially for the Tribuna (whose octagonal shape it repeats), it has been returned to its place in the center of the room, adorned with important pantings (such as Raphael's *St. John* and Franciabigio's *Virgin of the Well* which by 1589 were already hanging here) and ancient statues (such as *Scythian flaying Marsyas,* school of Pergamon, 3rd-2nd cent. B.C., the *Wrestlers,* Greek, 2nd cent. B.C. and the famous *Medici Venus,* a Greek copy of the 4th cent. B.C. original).

**Wrestlers,** 2nd century B.C. Greek art; below: **St. John the Baptist in the desert,** by *Raphael*;
**Portrait of Cosimo the Elder,** by *Jacopo Pontormo*.

**Scythian preparing to flay Marsyas** or **"the knife grinder"**, marble statue, school of Pergamon, 3rd-2nd century B.C.

Right: **top of the table inlaid with semi-precious stones**, designed by *Jacopo Ligozzi*.

Four portraits by *Agnolo Bronzino*. Above: **Girl with a book; Isabella dei Medici;** below: **Lucrezia Panciatichi; Giovanni dei Medici as a child.**

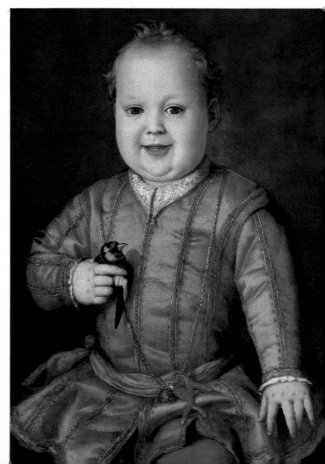

**Eleonor of Toledo and her son Giovanni,** by *Agnolo Bronzino.*

## Bronzino (1503-1572)

Agnolo Allori, better known as Bronzino, was just twenty when he joined forces with a fellow Mannerist painter Pontormo. The team worked in the Certosa in Galluzzo, Santa Felicita in Florence, and the Villa Medici at Poggio a Caiano. By the time he was appointed official court painter to Cosimo I, in 1539, Bronzino's style had already taken on the intellectual abstractness for which he is so famous, especially as a portrait painter.

*Eleonora di Toledo*, daughter of the Spanish viceroy in Naples, was just 17 and renowned for her beauty when she wed Cosimo dei Medici in 1539. In this portrait dated around 1545, she is portrayed in an elaborate cut-velvet evening gown and adorned with splendid jewels. Her perfect oval face appears sculpted in alabaster rather than painted, glowing like a polished gemstone from the plain, squalid dark blue background. Beside her stands her son Giovanni, the future Medici cardinal.

**Madonna and Child** and **Crucifixion with Mary Magdalene,** both by *Luca Signorelli*; opposite:
**Virgin and Child with two saints,** by *Pietro Perugino.*

# Luca Signorelli (c. 1445-1523)

Born in Cortona near Arezzo which practically borders on the region of Umbria, Signorelli's style was influenced by the clear tones favored by his fellow Tuscan Piero della Francesca and the melancholy atmosphere typical of the Umbrian painter Perugino but render more dynamic and sculptural by the influence of Florentine masters, especially Antonio del Pollaiolo. Signorelli's most famous works include paintings, altarpieces, and frescoes, the most famous of all being the fresco cycle in the San Brizio Chapel in the Cathedral of Orvieto which Vasari describes as "all the stories about the end of the world (being represented) with bizarre and capricious invention."

The painting of the *Virgin and Child*, was painted around 1490 for Lorenzo di Pierfrancesco dei Medici. The dark hues in the tondo, reflected in the grisaille frame, reveal the influence of Leonardo, while the graceful nude shepherd figures behind the sculptural Virgin and idyllic landscape in the backgrorund give the painting a peaceful, somewhat archaic feeling.

# Perugino (1446-1523)

Although Pietro Vannucci, known as Perugino, was influenced by Piero della Francesca, Verrocchio, Signorelli, and Pollaiolo his style is quite different from theirs. His works exude a sense of languid mysticism which he obtains by setting graceful, somewhat melancholy figures in peaceful, luminous landscapes. Despite the fact the Perugino's activity continued well into the 16th century, his style never evolved, even though many important artistic innovations were then being introduced by his more advanced contemporaries. As a result, his later works are little more than repetitions of a well-known formula and thus lack vigor and inspiration.

This *Virgin and Child* was painted for the church of San Domenico in Fiesole in 1493, as we learn from the inscription along the base: PETRUS PERUSINUS PINXIT A.D. MCCCCLXXXXIII. The figures are placed in strict symmetry in the foreground against a series of archways framing a cloudless sky at twilight. The delicately modeled faces all bear subtle expressions of melancholy.

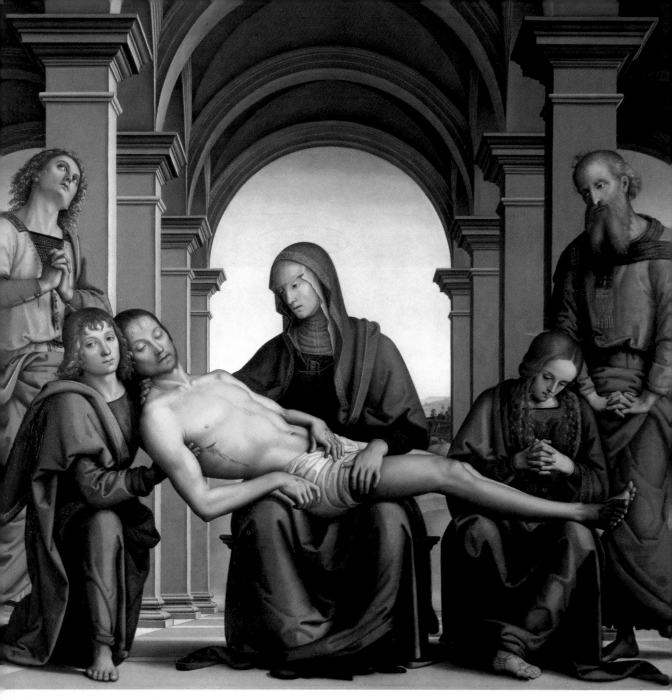

**Pietà,** by *Pietro Perugino.*

**Prayer in the Orchard,** by *Pietro Perugino.*

**Sacred Allegory,** by *Giovanni Bellini*; opposite: **Judgment of Solomon,** by *Giorgione*.

## Giovanni Bellini (c. 1430-1516)

The foremost 15th century Venetian painter, Giovanni Bellini trained in the studios of his father, Jacopo, whose style was charmingly archaic, and Gentile da Fabriano, the International Style master. Soon after, however, he come into contact with the new Renaissance style as practiced by Mantegna, turning Mantegna's formal rigor and rather cold gemlike palette into lyrical images rendered in warm, suffused tones. Giovanni was also influenced by the stately art of Piero della Francesca from whom he derived his fautless perspective and treatment of figures as solid monumental forms.

The *Sacred Allegory*, probably painted c. 1490, entered the Uffizi collection in 1793 as part of an exchange with the imperial collections of Vienna, and is one of Bellini's best known works, although what it represents is a mystery. An atmosphere of enchanted calm emanates from the natural setting of glimmering water, craggy cliffs, and a limpid sky, which dominates the painting. This feeling, at once warm and undefinable, envelops the whole, almost as if the figures were actually bathed in the soft colors of the setting sun.

## Giorgione (1477/78-1510)

Giorgione is the painter who, starting off from the sculptural forms of Giovanni Bellini, set Venetian art on the path to the pure, warm shades of color epitomized in the masterpieces of Titian. Giorgione's art is softer, more delicate and dreamy, just as you imagine an old-fashioned romantic. Unfortunately, Giorgione's premature death in the great plague which raged in Venice in 1510 clipped the wings to his soaring flights of imagination. As a matter of fact, few of his works have come down to us, as the Commission on Public Health of the Venetian Republic ordered that his belongings be burned as a health measure. Those surviving include the Sleeping Venus in Dresden, the Philosphers in Vienna, and the Tempest in the Accademia in Venice (the meaning of this latter work is obscure and the subject of great debate).

This *Judgment of Solomon*, with its companion piece, the Test of Fire, is a youthful work, perhaps dating from the time Giorgione was still apprenticed to Campagnola. The spacious tree-dotted landscape, full of atmosphere and great vitality, definitely reveals the presence of Giorgione's hand.

**Adoration of the Magi,** by *Albrecht Dürer*.

## Albrecht Dürer (1471-1528)

Dürer, the foremost 16th century German artist, was born in Nuremberg, although his father, a goldsmith, was actually a Hungarian. The rudiments of art, including how to use engraver's tools, were taught him by his father, and in fact he started his career as an engraver. Dürer's frequent travels and thus his constant exposure to Italian and German art, greatly influecend him, so that the early impact of Flemish painting was considerably weakened and his style soon revealed a sculptural quality and draughtsmanship, exceptional for a German artist of the time. He was especially attracted by the Italian Renaissance painters' emphasis on human anatomy, and he had occasion to observe, admire, and recall the works of Mantegna and Bellini, as is evident from the *Adoration of the Magi*. Here, in keeping with the tradition of Northern European painting, humans, objects, and nature are all attributed equal importance. On the other hand, the grandiosity of the composition and sensitivity in treating color are new elements in Dürer's work.

## Albrecht Altdorfer (1480-1538)

Altdorfer is the most important painter of the Danube School, one of the best-known artistic movements of the 16th century. In the works turned out by the school – undoubtedly romantic in style – we find a predominance of extensive landscape in which the sky and the whole atmosphere take part in the action as much or at times even more than the human figures.

The Life of St. Florian panels originally belonged to a great altarpiece painted for the church of St. Florian in Linz. Sections of the altarpiece are now in the museums of Berlin, Nuremberg, and Melk, in addition to the Uffizi which owns the Martyrdom of St. Florian as well as this remarkable *Departure*. Here the skeleton-like branches of the trees dramatically reach out toward the cold eerily-lit sky against a background of stark mountains. Yet the scene seems to exude a strong sense of melancholy accompanying the youthful saint towards his martyrdom, despite the metallic colors of the garments and the bright hues of the whole.

**Departure of St. Florian,** by *Albrecht Altdorfer*.

**Baptism of Christ,** by *Andrea del Verrocchio*.

## Andrea del Verrocchio (1435-1488)

Primarily a sculptor, Verrocchio trained the whole generation of late 15th - early 16th century Florentine artists in his workshop. Verrocchio's paintings are some-times a bit stiff, maybe because he could not bear to rid his figures of the metallic plasticity of his sculpture.

In this *Baptism of Christ*, however, the harsh effect is alleviated by the gentle brushstroke of Verrocchio's apprentice, Leonardo da Vinci, who added a touch of delicate shading to the forms.

**Annunciation;** below: **Adoration of the Magi,** both by *Leonardo da Vinci*.

# Leonardo da Vinci (1452-1519)

After completing his training in the workshop of Verrocchio, Leonardo laid the foundations for 16th century painting twenty years ahead of time. The new art forms and compositional patterns he invented became the canons and basic principles of painting lasting well into the 17th century. Leonardo perceived life as continous change caught in the act of becoming, and as such he represented it. He achieved this effect by his famous *sfumato*, a contourless distribution of light and shade, with the result that both figures and objects seem to dissolve into the brightly lit atmosphere around them. Later developments were the use of pyramidal composition, a new interpretation of light, as well as studies into nature in the broadest sense, especially man himself.

This *Annunciation* painted for the Monastery of Monteoliveto in Florence came to the Uffizi in 1870. A youthful work (c. 1470-1475), it still follows the traditional early 15th century compositional scheme along a single picture plane with a landscape in the background shown in perspective. Yet Leonardo's future development is already foreshadowed by the luminous treatment of the mountains and the mysterious half-smile on the Virgin's face.

This *Adoration of the Magi* is another of Leonardo's early works. Commissioned by the monks of San Donato at Scopeto in 1481, it was still unfinished when Leonardo moved to Milan. Despite the fact that he left it little more than a sketch, it already reveals several innovations: the *sfumato*, the intense light-shade contrasts, the pyramidal composition, and a scientific description of the flora and archeological elements.

67

**Rest in the Flight to Egypt;** opposite: **Adoration of the Child,** both by *Correggio*.

# Correggio (1489-1534)

Antonio Allegri, known as Correggio after his birth-place was influenced by Emilian and Venetian school painting as well as by the Tuscan school vis-à-vis his contemporaries, Michelangelo and Leonardo. The mixture of such multiple sources resulted in a completely new style characterized by the use of intense light and shade

contrasts, a rich palette of bright colors, and harmonious compositional patterns in canvases animated by figures of goddesses, cherubs, and Virgin Marys.

In this early *Rest on the flight to Egypt*, Correggio places the figures in a diagonal compositional scheme which he will continue to use throughout his mature period in his most famous paintings. Independently of the religious theme, the figures are portrayed before the shadowy wood without the slightest trace of sorrow.

The Second Corridor; left: **Girl preparing for dance**, copy from a 3rd century B.C. Hellenistic original; opposite, top: **detail of the fresco on the ceiling of the Second Corridor**; bottom: **Boy with a thorn**, Roman copy from a 2nd-1st century B.C. Hellenistic original; **bust of Antinous**, Roman art, Hadrian's period.

# THE SECOND CORRIDOR

The second corridor overlooks, on one side, the Arno and the hill of Forte di Belvedere and on the other the Piazzale degli Uffizi with Palazzo Vecchio acting as a stupendous backdrop. Among the important Roman sculptures exhibited are the *Boy removing a thorn*, two seated *matrons*, a huge sarcophagus with the *Fall of Phaeton*, and a porphyry fragment of a *she-wolf*.

The ceiling frescoes, of later date, portray the glories of Florentine saints.

The Third Corridor; left: **marble statue of Hercules.**

## THE THIRD CORRIDOR

At the beginning of the third corridor is a picture window looking out on the Arno, Ponte Vecchio, and the other Florentine bridges all the way down to the Cascine Park, and the churches on the left bank of the Arno. Again, sculpture is displayed, beginning with the two figures of *Marsyas hanging by his hands*. According to tradition, one was restored in the 15th century by Verrocchio and the other is said to have been retouched by Michelangelo. At the far end, right in front of the window-door leading to the terrace of the Loggia dell'Orcagna is a marble group representing *Laocoön and his sons*, a 16th century copy by Baccio Bandinelli of the original Roman sculpture preserved in the Vatican museum.

Just below the ceilings of the three corridors are

**Slain Marsyas,** copy from a 3rd century B.C. Hellenistic original; top right: **Laocoön and his children,** 16th century copy by *Baccio Bandinelli*; bottom right: **Bacchus with a young Satyr,** Roman copy from a Greek original of the end of the 4th century B.C.; following pages: **view from the windows of the Second Corridor.**

approximately 450 portraits of famous people. Collectively known as the Gioviana and post-Gioviana collections, they were executed by Cristofano dell'Altissimo (active from 1564 to 1605) and others (anonymous) up until the early 19th century. The original collection was commissioned by Cosimo I who wanted copies of the set that the historian Paolo Giovio kept at his estate on Lake Como (later lost).

**Holy Family,** also known as **Doni Tondo,** by *Michelangelo*.

## Michelangelo Buonarroti (1475-1564)

Painter, sculptor, architect, and poet, Michelangelo rose to the heights of human intellect and dominated all of 16th century art. He treated form in a such a way that the effect was both sculptural and dynamic, in keeping not only with his Florentine heritage, but also with his personal convinction that a painting's "worth is judged by how close it comes to (resembling) relief".

This painting portraying the *Holy Family* is known as the Doni Tondo since it was commissioned on occasion of Agnolo Doni's marriage to Maddalena Strozzi in 1506. It is the oldest surviving painted work by Michelangelo. Treated more as a sculpture than a painting, the group of the Holy Family is conceived in a spiraling movement which, from the Virgin's kness projecting in the foreground, extends up to the curly-haired sturdy Babe. The male nudes in the background, perhaps inspired by paintings by Luca Signorelli, are treated as if to simulate a monochrome bas-relief.

Above: **Cherub playing a lute,** by *Rosso Fiorentino*; left: **detail of the Doni Tondo,** by *Michelangelo*; below: **Moses defending the daughters of Jetro,** by *Rosso Fiorentino*.

## Rosso Fiorentino (1495-1540)

Giovanni Battista di Jacopo nicknamed "Il Rosso" (the redhead) because of the color of his hair, was a real non-conformist and the most original of the Tuscan Mannerists. His intellectual search for a new pictorial language led him to alternately emphasize form and color effects. The results, while not always consistent, were often quite original. Summoned to the court of François I of France in 1530, he was commissioned to decorate the Galerie de Fontainebleau, thus actively contributing to the spread of Italian Mannerism in France.

*Moses defending the daughters of Jethro*, one of Fiorentino's most important and complex pictures, was most likely painted around 1523, right before the artist left for a trip to Rome. On his return he would again fall under the spell of Michelangelo, but in this work Michelangelo's influence is wholly superficial, in that the movement of the figures appears to be suspended in time with the result that the overall effect is of an inaly of precious marbles.

**Leone X and cardinals Giulio dei Medici and Luigi dei Rossi,** by *Raphael*.

## Raphael (1483-1520)

As a native of Urbino, Raphael spent his early years surrounded by the classical Renaissance art of Laurana, Piero della Francesca and Paolo Uccello, all of whom were active in the highly intellectual court of Urbino, and they, together with the lovely countryside of his native Umbria and Sandro Botticelli, were his earliest influences. Later, when he went for formal training in Perugino's studio, he assimilated the art of perspective, as well as a feeling for balanced, harmonious composition. In Florence, struck by Leonardo's work, new elements such as the use of the *sfumato* technique and far-reaching landscapes came into his work, while his superb use of color, a result of Venetian influence, adds a range of lovely tones to his perfect, serene figures.

This *Self-portrait* is definitely an early work, probably painted during his 1506-1508 stay in Florence. Although a bit of nostalgia for the delicate Umbrian style is evident in the treatment of the head, the three quarters pose and draughtmanship are anything but old fashioned. Color is superbly used, especially in the subtle contrast of the various blacks against the enchanting golden flesh tones of the youth.

**Self-portrait,** by *Raphael*.

Right: **Virgin of the Goldfinch,** by *Raphael*.

The *Madonna del Cardellino*, dated 1506, was commissioned by Vincenzo Nasi, a wealthy Florentine and painted in Florence. Leonardo's influence is clearly visible in the pyramidal composition and use of *sfumato*, which here seems to envelop the solid forms, softening everything, and creating a delicate, luminous effect.

## Andrea del Sarto (1486-1531)

The art movement dominating the 16th, century after Michelangelo's death, known as Mannerism, was an attempt to fuse form as conceived by Michelangelo with color as conceived by Raphael. The artist who came closest to achieving this was Andrea del Sarto, whose work also reveals the influence of Leonardo. His huge canvases are peopled with solid sculptural figures set in

**Birth of St. John the Baptist,** by *Jacopo Pontormo*; opposite: **Madonna delle Arpie,** by *Andrea del Sarto.*

shadow that, unlike Leonardo's, is tinted rather than grey, and his palette abounds in warm tones. In fact, Andrea was so successful in harmoniously blending the various influences in his work that he was referred to as the "faultless painter".

The *Madonna delle Arpie* got its name from the Harpies sculpted on the corners of the pedestal supporting the figure of the Virgin, which also bears the artist's signature and the date 1517. The monumental quality of the figures is clearly a result of the influence of Michelangelo. The work was commissioned for the Convent of San Francesco in Florence.

## Pontormo (1491-1555)

Jacopo Carrucci, called Pontormo after his birthplace, is one of the most striking of the Tuscan Mannerists. A pupil of Andrea del Sarto, he later came under the direct influence of Michelangelo and Dürer whose engravings were already in circulation throughout Europe. Restless, temperamental, and a loner by nature, he endowed his paintings with a dynamic vitality which at times becomes exasperatedly dramatic and creates an effect of profound

**Virgin and Child with St. Jerome and St. Francis,** by *Jacopo Pontormo*; opposite: **Supper at Emmaus,** also by *Pontormo*.

melancholy. Many of his fine portraits, though bearing these traits, are more harmonious and less jarring.

The influence of Dürer, which his contemporaries, especially Vasari, judged deplorable, is clearly evident in this *Supper at Emmaus* which was directly inspired by the German master's engravings of the so-called "Small Passion". Pontormo painted it in 1525 for the Carthusian Monastery at Galluzzo, a small town near Florence, in which three years before he had sought refuge from the plague then reaping victims in the city. The painting is exceptionally advanced for its time, both with regards to the treatment of light, which seems to foreshadow Caravaggio, and the attention to details such as the table settings, which foreshadows 17th century painting.

**Venus of Urbino**; below: **Portrait of Eleonora Gonzaga della Rovere**; right: **Flora,** three works by *Titian*.

## Titian (1490?-1576)

Titian, undoubtedly the greatest pupil of Giorgione and Giovanni Bellini, was the greatest figure of 16th century Venetian art. In his hands, Giorgione and Bellini's delicate lyricism became intense drama. His rich palette and the intense warm glow bathing his pictures became the model for all of Venetian coloring. Also, as his view of the world broadened, his figures seem to expand in unison, getting larger, more powerful, more heroic all the time — perhaps en echo of Michelangelesque grandiosity.

*Flora* which was acquired by the Uffizi in the 1793 exchange with the Imperial Gallery of Vienna, is a youthful work, full of bright colors, in which, however, the influence of Giorgione's soft, modulated tones is still evident, especially in the treatment of the figure's golden flesh, spotlighted drapery, and dreamy gaze.

The *Venus of Urbino*, on the other hand, was painted in 1538 in the artist's mature period. Commissioned by Guidobaldo da Montefeltro, it came into the Medici collection in the 17th century as part of the della Rovere testament. It reveals the painter at the height of his artistic powers: a warm light plays over the glowing flesh of the sensual reclining figure of Venus, set off by sumptuous brocades, satiny sheets, and rich velvet hangings, and creates the dusky glow pouring in from the Venetian lagoon visible beyond the window.

**Death of Adonis,** by *Sebastiano del Piombo*; left: **Rest in the Flight to Egypt,** by *Dosso Dossi*.

## Sebastiano Luciani, known as Del Piombo (1485-1547)

The name del Piombo (roughly, "of the seal") comes from the fact that for many years he held the position of "papal abbreviator". Born and educated in Venice, he never forgot the colors of the lagoons which he absorbed from the paintings of Giorgione, even though throughout his long stay in Rome he was in close contact with the art of Michelangelo whom he greatly admired. In addition, he was influenced by Raphael who in turn was also influenced by the Piombo's own rich palette.

In the Uffizi *Death of Adonis*, one of th artist's masterpieces, these two tendencies are harmoniously blended. The romantic effect of the dusky tones enveloping the Doge's Palace and the melancholy trees in the background against the spacious sky reveal the influence of Giorgione, while the fleshy, extremely sculptural female nudes recall the grandiosity of Michelangelo.

**Witchcraft,** by *Dosso Dossi.*

# Dosso Dossi (1489?-1542)

Born in Ferrara, Dosso Dossi evidently came under the spell of Venetian colorism which had greatly affected all Ferrarese painting. Mostly influenced by Giorgione and Bellini, he was also affected by the great art of Titian, especially the Venetian master's powerful yet delicate brushstroke. Another influence was the imaginative streak of his contemporary, the writer Ariosto, who was at the court of the Dukes of d'Este, just as he was.

This is revealed in his *Witchcraft*, a late work, which is alive with glowing color and solid plasticism. The painting, purchased in Siena in 1665 by Cardinal Leopoldo dei Medici, originally hung in the Camerino degli Alabastri in the d'Este Palace in Ferrara. Full of imaginative and sensual touches (although the subject is a bit obscure), the painting reveals a lively skill in the rendering of the foreground still-life and the life-like portrait figures, which are so full of life we can almost picture them, still alive, going about their daily business in the Ferrara of today.

## Parmigianino (1503-1540)

Francesco Mazzola, called Parmigianino after his native town of Parma, studied under Correggio, although he was also influenced by Raphael. A skilled draughtsman and engraver, Parmigianino achieved a highly refined, extremely intellectual elegance in his painting style: elegant are his compositions, elegant is his subtle palette, and elegant are the poses of his figures.

The *Madonna dal collo lungo* (Virgin with the long neck) begun in 1534, was still unfinished when Parmigianino died, just 37, in 1540. It is one of the master's most representative paintings. The utterly graceful, slightly simpering Virgin with her elongated body looks more like a sophisticated lady or a pagan goddess than the Mother of God, who unlike this elegant creature, is customarily portrayed full of sorrowful foreboding for the tragic fate of her Son, here shown sleeping outstretched on her lap. Moreover, just as the marble colonnade in the background, the figure of the Virgin appears to have been sculpted rather than painted on the canvas.

## Paolo Caliari, known as Veronese (1528-1588)

Veronese is considered one of the greatest Venetian painters, even though he was actually born in Verona. He was the painter most influenced by the new Florentine Mannerist style, but at the same time the one whose work most abounds with pale luminous colors of the Venetian lagoon. In his pictures, great, intesely blue, cloud-dotted skies open over the rooftops of Venetian palaces. Florid

**Virgin with the long neck,** by *Parmigianino*.

**Esther and Ahasuerus;** right:
**Holy Family with St. Barbara,**
both by *Paolo Veronese*.

figures are set in regal compositions
and shown from skillfully foreshortened views.

The *Holy Family*, originally hung in
Casa Vidman in Venice, was bought in
1654 by Cardinal Leopoldo dei Medici.
One of Veronese's finest late works,
painted when contact with Tintoretto
rendered his palette even duskier than
before, the picture reflects the warmth
of the lovely Child. The figure of St.
Barbara, clearly the focal point of the
composition, is rendered in bright colors, especially the rich shades of her
long blond hair and golden stripes of
her dress. She seems to symbolize the
opulence of the Serenissima, republic
of the Doges.

**Leda and the swan,** by *Tintoretto*; opposite: **St. Francis and St. John the Evangelist,** by *El Greco*.

## Domenico Theotocopoulos, known as El Greco (1541-1614)

Despite the fact that there are few works representing the Spanish school in the Uffizi, those on display are all masterpieces and, except for the two Velasquez self-portraits, recent acquisitions. Actually, it is strange that the Medicis who were so closely linked to the Spanish politically should have shown so little interest in Spain's art. Domenico Theotocopoulos, better known as El Greco, one of the foremost Spanish school painters, was actually born in Crete, although he lived for years in Toledo where he was called "the Greek" ("El Greco"). For two years he lived in Venice studying under Titian. Certainly one of the Venetian master's outstanding pupils, he was also one of those most influenced by his colorism and use of strong lightshade contrasts, a trait which would later become one of the hallmarks of the El Greco style. In fact, following his training period, El Greco went off to Toledo where he continued to develop his elongated, suffering, sorrowing figures which seem to be submerged in space in a kind of unreal life.

This painting of *Sts. Francis and John the Evangelist*, originally part of thed Ruspoli Collection and purchased for the Uffizi by the state, dates from the artist's late period. It resembles a painting of the same subject preserved in the Prado, although the Uffizi version is finer. The sculptural quality of the figures has been pared down, while the different picture planes, all pointing upwards, are distinguishable mainly by color. Everything, from drapery to rocks and clouds, is rendered with great elegance in a pathetic atmosphere; a silent, inner dialogue is rendered thanks to the vibrant brushstroke of the painter who seems to be painting spirits rather than bodies.

## Jacopo Robusti, known as Tintoretto (1518-1594)

In Tintoretto, Central Italian Mannerism blends into the Venetian tradition. His style is dynamic and he uses lights to dazzle causing contours to disappear. His painting attempts to capture the effect of movement in the visualisation of a fleeting instant. His composition as in this late work of *Leda and the swan*, is never static, never symmetrical, never restful.

91

**Henry IV triumphantly entering Paris**; right: **Portrait of Isabella Brandt**, both by *Peter Paul Rubens*.

## Peter Paul Rubens (1577-1640)

Flemish by birth, Rubens studied the great masters of Antwerp, yet it was the unsuperable Italian art of the 16th and early 17th centuries that had the greatest impact on him when he took a study tour of Italy in his youth. His striking use of color and rich, vital style made him the outstanding Baroque painter in Flanders. In all his numerous works on subjects ranging from classical, mythological, and religious themes to portraits, he uses bright colors and radiant light to express a passionate joie de vivre — lived to the hilt — sometimes expressed as an explosion of dramatic excitement.

The portrait of the artist's first wife, *Isabella Brandt*, probably painted in 1324-1325, just before her death in 1626, is one of Rubens' finest. Set solidly into space, the figure of the woman, a half-smile poised on her lips, is illuminated by a soft light which, passing over the shiny material of her elaborate black gown, delicate lace cuffs, lace collar, and red curtain behind her, adds a tender sensuality to her flesh and a crystalline purity to her jewels.

The Niobe Room and, in the foreground, the Medici Vase, neo-attic; right: Boy playing cards, by *Jean-Baptiste Chardin*.

## Jean-Baptiste Chardin (1699-1779)

The gallant, refined, affected nature of 18th century Parisian high society was reflected in the prevailing painting style of the times, characterized by extravagance and flights of imagination. Chardin was one of the few who turned his back on Baroque excess and instead concentrated his attention on depicting middle class people surrounded by their simple household objects which, singled out and painstakingly portrayed, are themselves reflections of the bourgeoisie's tranquil lifestyle. No stylistic evolution is discernable in Chardin's oeuvre which consists of still-lifes, portraits, and interiors showing people as they are going about their daily routine, yet everything he painted was viewed through fond eyes, as Chardin himself often said "with feeling more than color".

The *Boy playing cards* is one of the Uffizi's more recent acquisitions (1951). Intent on his card game, the boy sits impeccably dressed in a smart suit. The canvas is signed and a replica by Chardin himself is to be found in the Metropolitan Museum in New York.

**View of the harbor of St. Mark's in Venice,** by *Canaletto*; below: **Seascape with an archway,** by *Francesco Guardi.*

## Antonio Canal, known as Canaletto (1697-1768)

One of the greatest of the 18th century Italian landscapists and one of the most skilled Venetian painters, Canaletto portrayed realistic views in a poetic style, whereby creating a wholly imaginative effect. He especially loved to paint views of Venice, depicting all its well-known and not so well-known corners with precision so painstaking it sometimes borders on the photographic. Nevertheless, his realism never gets excessive, thanks to his typically Venetian love for light, which in this painting plays over the elaborate decorative architecture of the palace and the Basilica, the city's throbbing hearts. The light is fraught with subtle tremors that vibrate over the water and golden sky, which almost seem to change from minute to minute, hour to hour.

**Venus, satyr and cherubs,** or **Bacchante,** by *Annibale Carracci.*

## Francesco Guardi (1712-1793)

When mention is made of 18th century Venetian painting, the name of Giovanni Battista Tiepolo immediately comes to mind, although the great landscapists, the so-calledd *vedutisti*, Canaletto and Guardi foremost among them, occupy just as important a position as Tiepolo. Francesco Guardi, the most modern of all, goes beyond just a trite reproduction of reality, and recreates nature using only light and color to achieve his effects. His imagination serves to endow objects with such consistency that at times the air itself seem to possess a density of its own and, as a result, his views, mostly imaginary landscapes, are full of poetic melancholy.

This *Seascape with an archway*, together with the other small canvas, Village and a canal, are late works, executed when the artist's style had become so delicate that his brushsrokes practically disintegrate in the delicate coloring of the light, water, and sky.

## Annibale Carracci (1560-1609)

Founder, together with is brother, Agostino, and cousin, Ludovico, of the Academy of the Incamminati in Bologna, Annibale Carracci breathed new life into late 16th century Italian painting which was on the way to becoming just a lifeless re-elaboration of early 16th century Mannerism. Imaginative and vigorous, he skillfully welded elements from the Venetian, Emilian, and Roman schools into a complex serene blend, sprinkling his pictures with references to classical mythology (from which he derived the subject matter for his greatest undertaking, the decoration of the Farnese Gallery in Rome).

In this youthful work, the so-called *Bacchante*, the overriding influence is clearly that of Titian. The pagan scene, perfectly suited to the artist's temperament, of a nude young woman shown from the back and framed by a satyr and two putti, is masterfully executed with Carracci's characteristic exuberant verve.

*Sacrifice of Isaac*; below: **Medusa head**; opposite: **Bacchus**, three works by *Caravaggio*.

## Caravaggio (1573-1610)

Caravaggio, born in Caravaggio, Lombardy (northern Italy) took an almost controversial stand when he championed the need for art to return to reality. This was in opposition to the prevailing movement of the day which was an offshoot of the intellectual art practised by the Carraccis. Caravaggio in fact lived most of his brief life in Rome and there he produced his impressive canvases. The *Bacchus* was painted in 1589 shortly after Caravaggio moved to Rome. The mythological deity is depicted with simplicity as a puffy Roman teenager, glazy-eyed from too much wine, who for fun has decked himself out with a garland of vine leaves. A bright light floods the picture, highlighting the youth's flabby flesh, the crumpled bedsheet, the fruit basket, and the wine carafe of crystalline solidity.

The *Sacrifice of Isaac* also dates from Caravaggio's early years. It has the same compelling quality about it, although here the effect is much more dramatic as we follow the story from Isaac's fearful shriek on the right to Abraham caught in the instant that the angel, of classic beauty, stops him. The landscape in the background is clear proof of the influence of Giorgione.

**Self-portrait as a young man,** by *Rembrandt van Rijn*.

**Self-portrait as an old man,** by *Rembrandt van Rijn*.

## Rembrandt van Rijn (1606-1669)

Rembrandt was born in Leyden in 1606. Although his father, a wealthy miller, would have liked his son to devote himself to Humanistic studies, young Rembrandt had his heart set on studying painting and began his training under a Dutch artist, Peter Lastmann. His style soon developed into something completely different from his master's and it was not long before his immense creativity and technical skill brought him wealth and fame. At the height of his prosperity, a chain of deaths in his family and financial setbacks struck him one after another until he himself died practically a pauper in 1669.

This *Self-portrait* painted c. 1634 was acquired by the Gerini family, before passing to the Uffizi in 1818. The pensive figure of the artist enveloped in warm-toned shadows is accented by light reflected from the metal ruff and chain onto his face below the dark beret, blond hair, and fur cloak thrown over his shoulder.

LIFT

**The Boar,** Roman copy of a 3rd century B.C. Hellenistic original; below: **the staircase leading down to the Vasari Corridor.**

The Vasari Corridor.

# THE CORRIDOIO VASARIANO

The name *Vasariano* comes from the architect of the Uffizi, Giorgio Vasari. Vasari received the commission from Grandduke Cosimo I dei Medici in March of 1565. The project was supposed to be completed in time for the wedding of the heir to the title, the future Francesco I, to Joan of Austria, sister of Emperor Maximilian I, scheduled for December of that year. It was to be a kind of elevated road connecting the palace, Palazzo Pitti, to the Uffizi and, in turn, by means of an overhead passageway crossing Via della Ninna, to Palazzo Vecchio. In September of the same year, Vasari unveiled his finished work. It had involved extremely hard work, especially along the section by the Arno where it practically spans the river (the arcade known as "Archibusieri"). The *corridoio* then turns left, passing right through Ponte Vecchio, private houses, and

the church of Santa Felicita, coming out in the Boboli Gardens alongside the grotto which Buontalenti later designed for Francesco I and ending by the secondary staircase of Palazzo Pitti.

The only ones to object to the corridor's passing through their homes were the Mannellis and, since, according to Cosimo "everyone's master of his own home". Vasari had to solve the problem by designing an outer balcony sustained by huge brackets. Thus, the wall of the corridor, extremely narrow at that point, is actually the stone facing of the Mannelli Tower. During restoration carried out in 1973, the balcony designed by Buontalenti inside the church of Santa Felicita and used as the royal chapel throughout the 17th century, was brought back to light. From this vantage point the family and court of the grandduke could listen to Mass and the other church

Interior of the church of Santa Felicita from a balcony in the Vasari Corridor; below: view
from a window in the Vasari Corridor facing onto the Ponte Vecchio.

**Portraits of some members of the Medici family,** school of *Bronzino*, 16th century.

**View of the Uffizi and the Vasari Corridor from the outside** – *We are facing the far side of the Uffizi overlooking the Arno. Perhaps the least known, yet most monumental side, it extends along the Archibusieri arcade, as the most elevated stretch, "placed over*

services. The corridor actually became the fastest way for the Prince to get from his residence to his collections, the theater, the Uffizi, and Palazzo Vecchio, headquarters of the government of the grandduchy.

Only later were the works from the Classical period, tapestries, and drawings put on display and just before World War II the iconographic collection was set up. Finally, in 1973, the Self-portrait Collection, one of a kind in all the world, was hung along the corridor. The collection, started by Cardinal Leopoldo dei Medici, includes well-known works from the 14th century portraits of the Gaddis and covers all periods and schools, from Raphael and

*water and in air", as Vasari described the corridor which bears his name. Our glance follows it to the Ponte Vecchio, the bridge of the jewelers, over whose shops it passes on its way to Palazzo Pitti.*

Titian to Velasquez, Rembrandt, Rubens, Delacroix, Ingres, Fattori, right up to Marc Chagall. In 1976 Chagall, whose self-portrait is set in a vision of the Seine and Notre-Dame, seems to have revived the old tradition of famous artists donating their self-portraits to the Uffizi.

Along the first section of the corridor are Cara-vaggesque paintings and other major Italian and non-Italian 17th century paintings by such name painters as Lyss, Feti, Vanvitelli, Crespi, Rosalba Carriera, Batoni, and a host of others. At the end of Ponte Vecchio, on the Pitti side, is a statue of Cardinal Leopoldo, one of the finest works by Foggini, the 17th century Florentine sculptor.

**Self-portrait,** by *Jacques-Louis David*; **Self-portrait,** by *Antonio Canova*; below: **Self-portrait,** by *Diego Velazquez*; **Self-portrait,** by *Angelica Kauffmann*.

**Self-portrait,** by *Leonardo da Vinci*.

Self-portrait, by *Peter Paul Rubens*; opposite: **Self-portrait,** by *Gian Lorenzo Bernini*.

View of the Piazzale degli Uffizi with Palazzo Vecchio in the foreground.

# INDEX

# INDEX OF THE ARTISTS